Thread Bo

Double the pleasure of
bookmarks! Great for gifts, t
Stephens are all made usir

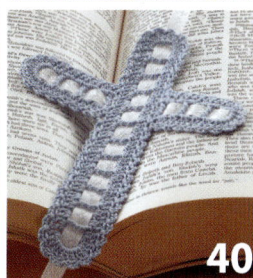

2

6

10

14

18

22

26

32

36

40

LEISURE ARTS, INC. • Maumelle, Arkansas

BIRDHOUSE BORDER

◖■▭▭▷ **EASY +**

Approximate Finished Size:
1⅞"w x 7"h (4.75 cm x 18 cm) (excluding fringe)

SHOPPING LIST

Thread (Lace Weight) 🧶 LACE 0
Crochet Thread, size 10
Purple Version
[350 yards (320 meters) per ball]:
☐ Purple - 10 yards (9 meters)
☐ Lavender - 7 yards (6.5 meters)
Variegated Version
[300 yards (274 meters) per ball]:
☐ 17 yards (15.5 meters)

Crochet Hook
☐ Steel hook, size 10 (1.3 mm)

To make the Bookmark using the chart on page 5, see Following Symbol Crochet Charts on page 46.

Rows 2-29: Ch 3 (**counts as first dc, now and throughout**), turn; dc in next dc and in each dc across.

Row 30: Ch 3, turn; dc in next dc and in each dc across changing to Lavender in last dc made *(Fig. 1)*.

Fig. 1

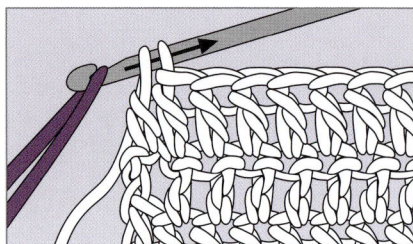

Note: Instructions are written for Purple Version. For Variegated Version, do **not** change colors or finish off at end of Row 30.

INSTRUCTIONS

With Purple, ch 12; place a marker in third ch from hook for Edging placement.

Row 1 (Wrong side)**:** Dc in fourth ch from hook (**3 skipped chs count as first dc)** and in each ch across: 10 dc.

Note: Loop a short piece of thread around the **back** of any stitch on Row 1 to mark **right** side and bottom.

EDGING

Rnd 1: Ch 4, do **not** turn; working in top of dc at end of rows, skip first 2 rows, (slip st in next row, ch 4, skip next row) across; working in free loops of beginning ch *(Fig. 2, page 46)*, slip st in marked ch, remove marker, ch 4, (skip next 2 chs, slip st in next ch, ch 4) 3 times; working in top of dc at end of rows, skip first row, slip st in next row, ch 4, (skip next row, slip st in next row, ch 4) across to last 2 rows, skip last 2 rows; working in sts across Row 30, slip st in first dc, (ch 4, skip next 2 dc, slip st in next dc) 3 times, ending in dc at base of beginning ch-4: 36 ch-4 sps.

Rnd 2: Slip st in next ch-4 sp, ch 3, (2 dc, ch 2, 3 dc) in same sp, ch 2, slip st in next ch-4 sp, ch 2, ★ (3 dc, ch 2) twice in next ch-4 sp, slip st in next ch-4 sp, ch 2; repeat from ★ around; join with slip st to first dc, finish off.

Cut five, 5" (12.5 cm) pieces of thread. Fold one strand in half. With **wrong** side facing and using hook, draw the folded end up through the center ch-2 sp at bottom of piece and pull the loose ends through the folded end; draw the knot up **tightly**. Repeat with the remaining 4 strands. Lay Bookmark flat on a hard surface and trim ends.

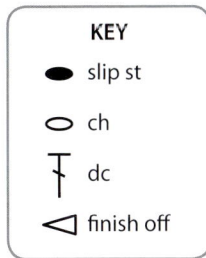

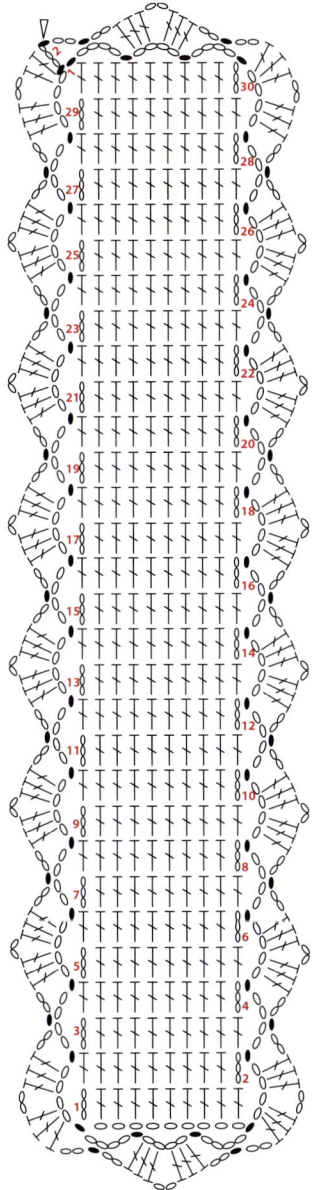

KEY

● slip st

○ ch

Ŧ dc

◁ finish off

BEAUTIFUL BUTTERFLY

■■□□ **EASY +**

Approximate Finished Size:
2"w x 1⅛"h (5 cm x 3 cm) (excluding ribbon)

SHOPPING LIST

Thread (Lace Weight) 0 LACE
Crochet Thread, size 10

Pink Version
[350 yards (320 meters) per ball]:
- ☐ Dk Pink - 4 yards (3.5 meters)
- ☐ Pink - 4 yards (3.5 meters)

Blue Variegated Version
[300 yards (274 meters) per ball]:
- ☐ 8 yards (7.5 meters)

Crochet Hook
- ☐ Steel hook, size 10 (1.3 mm)

Additional Supplies
- ☐ ⁵⁄₁₆"w (8 mm) Ribbon - 8" (20.5 cm) length
- ☐ ⅛"w (3 mm) Ribbon - 4" (10 cm) length
- ☐ ¼" (6 mm) Button
- ☐ Craft glue

To make the Bookmark using the chart on page 9, see Following Symbol Crochet Charts on page 46.

Note: Instructions are written for Pink Version. For Blue Variegated Version, do **not** finish off at end of Rnd 4. Begin Rnd 5 by slip stitching across to center of first ch-9 sp.

INSTRUCTIONS

With Dk Pink, ch 6; join with slip st to form a ring.

Rnd 1 (Right side)**:** Ch 3 (**counts as first dc**), 15 dc in ring; join with slip st to first dc: 16 dc.

Note: Loop a short piece of thread around any stitch to mark Rnd 1 as **right** side.

Rnd 2: Ch 1, sc in same st as joining, ch 5, skip next dc, ★ sc in next dc, ch 5, skip next dc; repeat from ★ around; join with slip st to first sc: 8 sc and 8 ch-5 sps.

Rnd 3: Ch 1, sc in same st as joining, ch 7, skip next ch-5 sp, ★ sc in next sc, ch 7, skip next ch-5 sp; repeat from ★ around; join with slip st to first sc.

Rnd 4: Ch 1, sc in same st as joining, ch 9, skip next ch-7 sp, ★ sc in next sc, ch 9, skip next ch-7 sp; repeat from ★ around; join with slip st to first sc, finish off.

Rnd 5: With **right** side facing, join Pink with slip st in any ch-9 sp; (ch 3, slip st in same sp) 8 times, ★ slip st in next ch-9 sp, (ch 3, slip st in same sp) 8 times; repeat from ★ around; join with slip st to first slip st, finish off.

Using photo as a guide:
Fold 1/8"w (3 mm) ribbon in half and glue cut ends together. Insert cut ends through beginning ring from **right** to **wrong** side; glue one side of cut ends to **wrong** side of piece. Glue one end of 5/16"w (8 mm) ribbon to cut end of 1/8"w (3 mm) ribbon.

Fold crocheted piece piece in half with **wrong** side together, having loop centered, and glue **wrong** side of piece to 5/16"w (8 mm) ribbon.
Glue button to center of folded edge. Allow glue to dry completely. Trim end as desired.

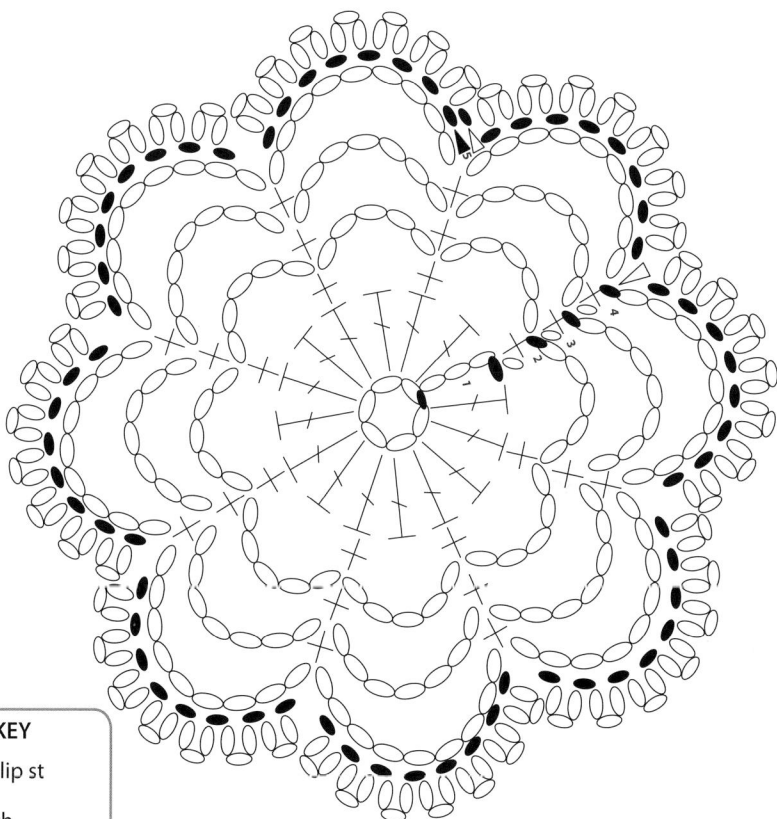

KEY
- ⬬ slip st
- ⬭ ch
- + sc
- ⊤ dc
- ◀ join
- ◁ finish off

LACY DREAM

■■□□ EASY +

Approximate Finished Size:
1¾"w x 6¾"h (4.5 cm x 17 cm) (excluding ribbon)

SHOPPING LIST

Thread (Lace Weight) **LACE 0**
Crochet Thread, size 10
[350 yards (320 meters) per ball]:
☐ 14 yards (13 meters)

Crochet Hook
☐ Steel hook, size 10 (1.3 mm)

Additional Supplies
☐ ³/₁₆"w (5 mm) Ribbon - 9" (23 cm) length

To make the Bookmark using the chart on page 13,
see Following Symbol Crochet Charts on page 46.

INSTRUCTIONS

Ch 77.

Foundation Row: Dc in eighth ch from hook, ★ ch 2, skip next 2 chs, dc in next ch; repeat from ★ across: 24 dc and 24 sps.

Rnd 1 (Right side)**:** Ch 3 (**counts as first dc, now and throughout**), do **not** turn; (dc, ch 3, 2 dc) in sp at end of Foundation Row, ch 2; working in sps of beginning ch, 2 dc in each of first 23 sps, (2 dc, ch 2, 2 dc) in sp at opposite end of Foundation Row, ch 3, (2 dc, ch 2, 2 dc) in same sp, 2 dc in each of next 23 ch-2 sps, ch 2; join with slip st to first dc: 104 dc and 6 sps.

Rnd 2: Slip st in next dc and in next ch-3 sp, ch 3, (dc, ch 3, 2 dc) in same sp, ch 2, (2 dc, ch 2) twice in next ch-2 sp, [skip next 3 dc, (dc, ch 2) twice in next dc] 11 times, skip next 4 dc, (2 dc, ch 2) twice in next ch-2 sp, (2 dc, ch 3, 2 dc) in next ch-3 sp, ch 2, (2 dc, ch 2) twice in next ch-2 sp, skip next 4 dc, [(dc, ch 2) twice in next dc, skip next 3 dc] 11 times, (2 dc, ch 2) twice in last ch-2 sp; join with slip st to first dc: 68 dc and 56 sps.

Rnd 3: Slip st in next dc, (slip st, ch 4) twice in each of next 3 sps, † skip next ch-2 sp, [(slip st, ch 4) twice in next ch-2 sp, skip next ch-2 sp] 11 times †, (slip st, ch 4) twice in each of next 5 sps, repeat from † to † once, (slip st, ch 4) twice in next ch-2 sp, (slip st, ch 4, slip st) in last ch-2 sp, ch 2, skip first slip st, hdc in next slip st at base of beginning ch-4 to form last ch-4 sp: 64 ch-4 sps.

Rnd 4: Ch 7, skip next ch-4 sp, ★ slip st in next ch-4 sp, ch 7, skip next ch-4 sp; repeat from ★ around; join with slip st to hdc at base of beginning ch-7, finish off.

Using photo as a guide, weave ribbon through sps on Foundation Row. Trim ends as desired.

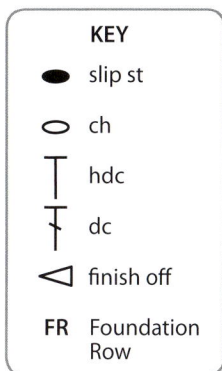

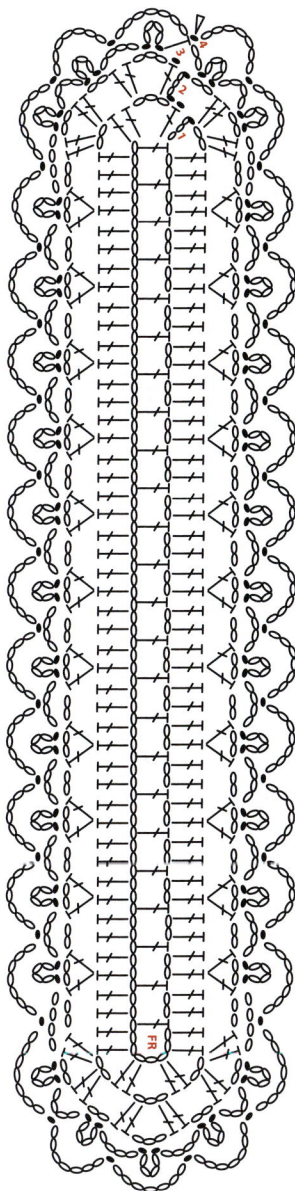

KEY	
●	slip st
○	ch
T	hdc
⊤	dc
◁	finish off
FR	Foundation Row

WOVEN CROSS

⬛⬛⬜⬜ **EASY +**

Approximate Finished Size:
2¾"w x 6⅜"h (7 cm x 16 cm)

SHOPPING LIST

Thread (Lace Weight) 🔟
Crochet Thread, size 10
[350 yards (320 meters) per ball]:
☐ 23 yards (21 meters)

Crochet Hook
☐ Steel hook, size 10 (1.3 mm)

Additional Supplies
☐ 1/16"w (2 mm) Ribbon - 7" (18 cm) length
☐ Craft glue

To make the Bookmark using the chart on page 17, see Following Symbol Crochet Charts on page 46.

INSTRUCTIONS

Ch 26.

Row 1 (Right side)**:** Dc in fourth ch from hook **(3 skipped chs count as first dc)** and in each ch across: 24 dc.

Note: Loop a short piece of thread around any stitch to mark Row 1 as **right** side.

Rows 2-4: Ch 3 **(counts as first dc, now and throughout)**, turn; dc in next dc and in each dc across.

Row 5: Ch 3, turn; dc in next 10 dc, ch 2, skip next 2 dc, dc in last 11 dc: 22 dc and one ch-2 sp.

Rows 6-18: Ch 3, turn; dc in next 10 dc, ch 2, skip next ch-2 sp, dc in last 11 dc.

Row 19: Ch 3, turn; dc in next 4 dc, (ch 2, skip next 2 dc, dc in next dc) twice, ch 2, skip next ch-2 sp, (dc in next dc, ch 2, skip next 2 dc) twice, dc in last 5 dc: 14 dc and 5 ch-2 sps.

Row 20: Ch 3, turn; dc in next 4 dc, (2 dc in next ch-2 sp, dc in next dc) twice, ch 2, skip next ch-2 sp, (dc in next dc, 2 dc in next ch-2 sp) twice, dc in last 5 dc: 22 dc and one ch-2 sp.

Rows 21-24: Ch 3, turn; dc in next 10 dc, ch 2, skip next ch-2 sp, dc in last 11 dc.

Row 25: Ch 3, turn; dc in next 10 dc, 2 dc in next ch-2 sp, dc in last 11 dc: 24 dc.

Rows 26-28: Ch 3, turn; dc in next dc and in each dc across.

Edging: Ch 5, turn; (slip st, ch 5, slip st) in first dc, ch 12, skip next 10 dc, slip st in next dc, (ch 5, slip st in same st) twice, ch 12, skip next 11 dc, slip st in last dc, (ch 5, slip st in same st) twice, ch 7; † working in end of rows, skip first 3 rows, slip st in next row, (ch 5, slip st in same row) twice, ch 7, [skip next 2 rows, slip st in next row, (ch 5, slip st in same row) twice, ch 7] 7 times, skip last 3 rows †; working in free loops of beginning ch *(Fig. 2, page 46)*, slip st in first ch, (ch 5, slip st in same st) twice, ch 12, skip next 10 chs, slip st in next ch, (ch 5, slip st in same ch) twice, ch 12, skip next 11 chs, slip st in next ch, (ch 5, slip st in same ch) twice, ch 7; repeat from † to † once; join with slip st to dc at base of beginning ch-5; finish off.

Using photo as a guide: Weave a 5" (12.5 cm) piece of ribbon through vertical ch-2 sps; fold each end to **wrong** side and glue in place. Weave remaining 2" (5 cm) piece of ribbon through horizontal ch-2 sps of Row 19; fold each end to **wrong** side and glue in place. Allow glue to dry completely.

Edging

KEY

●	slip st
○	ch
⊤	dc
◁	finish off

CROWNING TOUCH

◖■▢▭▭ **EASY +**

Approximate Finished Size:
2¼"w x 7¼"h (5.5 cm x 18.5 cm) (excluding ribbon)

SHOPPING LIST

Thread (Lace Weight) LACE 0
Crochet Thread, size 10
[350 yards (320 meters) per ball]:
☐ 20 yards (18.5 meters)

Crochet Hook
☐ Steel hook, size 10 (1.3 mm)

Additional Supplies
☐ 5/16"w (8 mm) Ribbon - 11" (28 cm) length

To make the Bookmark using the chart on page 21,
see Following Symbol Crochet Charts on page 46.

STITCH GUIDE

TREBLE CROCHET *(abbreviated tr)*
YO twice, insert hook in st indicated, YO and pull up a loop (4 loops on hook), (YO and draw through 2 loops on hook) 3 times.

INSTRUCTIONS
Ch 78.

Foundation Row: Tr in ninth ch from hook, ★ ch 2, skip next 2 chs, tr in next ch; repeat from ★ across: 24 tr and 24 sps.

Rnd 1 (Right side)**:** Ch 3 (**counts as first dc, now and throughout**), do **not** turn; dc in sp at end of Foundation Row, (ch 1, 2 dc in same sp) 3 times, working in sps of beginning ch, 2 dc in each of next 22 sps, 2 dc in sp at opposite end of Foundation Row, (ch 1, 2 dc in same sp) 5 times, 2 dc in each of next 22 ch-2 sps, (2 dc, ch 1) twice in last ch-2 sp; join with slip st to first dc: 112 dc and 10 ch-1 sps.

Rnd 2: Ch 7, (skip next ch-1 sp and next dc, slip st in next dc, ch 7) 3 times, (skip next 3 dc, slip st in next dc, ch 7) 11 times, skip next 2 dc and next ch-1 sp, slip st in next dc, ch 7, skip next dc and next ch-1 sp, slip st in next dc, ch 7, (skip next ch-1 sp and next dc, slip st in next dc, ch 7) twice, skip next ch-1 sp and next 2 dc, slip st in next dc, ch 7, (skip next 3 dc, slip st in next dc, ch 7) 11 times, skip next dc and next ch-1 sp, slip st in next dc, ch 7, skip last dc and last ch-1 sp; join with slip st to joining slip st at base of beginning ch-7: 32 ch-7 sps.

Rnd 3: (Slip st, ch 3, 2 dc, ch 3, 3 dc) in next ch-7 sp, ch 2, (3 dc in next ch-7 sp, ch 2) 15 times, (3 dc, ch 3, 3 dc) in next ch-7 sp, ch 2, (3 dc in next ch-7 sp, ch 2) across; join with slip st to first dc: 102 dc and 34 sps.

Rnd 4: Slip st in next dc, ch 1, ★ sc in next dc, ch 6, skip next ch-3 sp, sc in next dc, ch 6, (sc in next ch-2 sp, ch 6) 16 times, skip next 2 sts; repeat from ★ once **more**; join with slip st to first sc: 36 sc and 36 ch-6 sps.

Rnd 5: Ch 4, skip next 2 chs, (slip st, ch 4) twice in next ch, skip next 3 chs, slip st in next sc, ch 8, skip next ch-6 sp, ★ slip st in next sc, ch 4, skip next 2 chs, (slip st, ch 4) twice in next ch, skip next 3 chs, slip st in next sc, ch 8, skip next ch-6 sp; repeat from ★ around; join with slip st to joining slip st at base of beginning ch, finish off.

Using photo as a guide, weave ribbon through sps on Foundation Row.
Trim ends as desired.

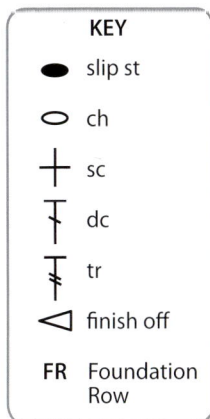

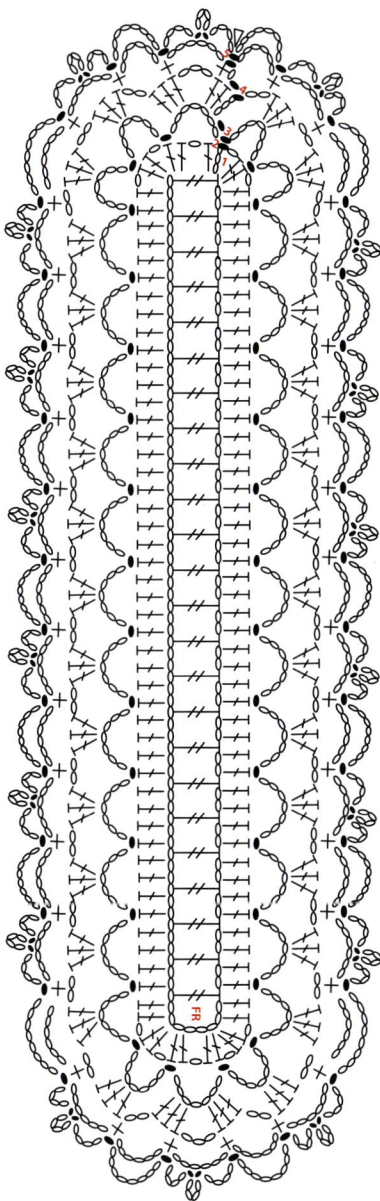

KEY	
⬤	slip st
○	ch
+	sc
†	dc
‡	tr
◁	finish off
FR	Foundation Row

FANCIFUL FANS

■■□□ EASY +

Approximate Finished Size:
1"w x 7¼"h (2.5 cm x 18.5 cm) (excluding fringe)

SHOPPING LIST

Thread (Lace Weight) **LACE 0**
Crochet Thread, size 10
[350 yards (320 meters) per ball **OR**
300 yards (274 meters) per ball]:
☐ 12 yards (11 meters)

Crochet Hook
☐ Steel hook, size 10 (1.3 mm)

To make the Bookmark using the chart on page 25,
see Following Symbol Crochet Charts on page 46.

INSTRUCTIONS

Ch 5; join with slip st to form a ring.

First Fan (Right side)**:** Ch 3 (**counts as first dc, now and throughout**), 8 dc in ring: 9 dc.

Note: Loop a short piece of thread around any stitch to mark First Fan as **right** side.

Next 17 Fans: Ch 5, slip st in fifth ch from hook to form a ring, ch 3, **turn**; 8 dc in ring.

You should now have a total of 18 Fans.

Edging: Ch 3, turn; skip first dc, slip st in next dc, (ch 3, slip st in next dc) 6 times, ★ ch 2, skip end of row and ring on next Fan, slip st in first dc on next Fan, (ch 3, slip st in next dc) 7 times; repeat from ★ 7 times **more**, ch 2, skip end of row and ring on last Fan, slip st in first dc on last Fan, (ch 3, slip st in next dc) twice, tie a scrap piece of thread around last ch-3 made for fringe placement, (ch 3, slip st in next dc) 5 times, † ch 2, skip ring and end of row on next Fan, slip st in first dc on next Fan, (ch 3, slip st in next dc) 7 times †; repeat from † to † 7 times **more**, ch 2; join with slip st to dc at base of beginning ch, finish off.

Cut five, 5" (12.5 cm) pieces of thread. Fold one strand in half. With **wrong** side facing and using hook, draw the folded end up through the marked ch-3 sp and pull the loose ends through the folded end; draw the knot up **tightly**. Repeat with the remaining 4 strands. Lay Bookmark flat on a hard surface and trim ends.

Marked → ch-3 sp

FIRST FAN

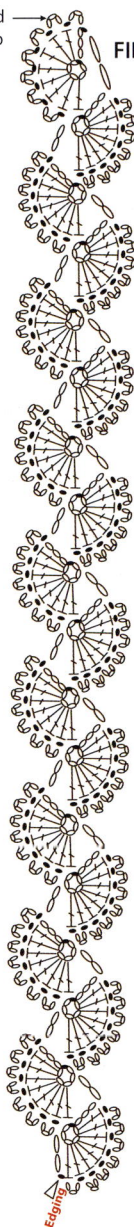

KEY
- ⬬ slip st
- ◯ ch
- ⊤ dc
- ◁ finish off

Edging

PRESSED FLOWERS

◀■■☐☐▷ EASY +

Approximate Finished Size:
1¼"w x 7½"h (3 cm x 19 cm) (excluding ribbon)

SHOPPING LIST

Thread (Lace Weight) 🧵 **0** LACE
Crochet Thread, size 10
[350 yards (320 meters) per ball]:
☐ Lavender - 5 yards (4.5 meters)
[300 yards (274 meters) per ball]:
☐ Variegated - 5 yards (4.5 meters)

Crochet Hook
☐ Steel hook, size 10 (1.3 mm)

Additional Supplies
☐ ⅝"w (16 mm) Ribbon - 11" (28 cm) length
☐ Craft glue

To make the Bookmark using the chart on page 31,
see Following Symbol Crochet Charts on page 46.

INSTRUCTIONS
FIRST FLOWER

With Lavender, ch 6; join with slip st to form a ring.

Rnd 1 (Right side)**:** Ch 3 (**counts as first dc**), 11 dc in ring; join with slip st to first dc: 12 dc.

Note: Loop a short piece of thread around any stitch to mark Rnd 1 as **right** side.

Rnd 2: Ch 3 (**counts as first dc**), dc in same st as joining, 2 dc in next dc and in each dc around; join with slip st to first dc: 24 dc.

Rnd 3: Ch 3, (slip st in next dc, ch 3)around; join with slip st to joining slip st at base of beginning ch-3, finish off: 24 ch-3 sps.

SECOND FLOWER

With Variegated, ch 6; join with slip st to form a ring.

Rnd 1 (Right side)**:** Ch 3 (**counts as first dc**), 11 dc in ring; join with slip st to first dc: 12 dc.

Note: Mark Rnd 1 as **right** side.

Rnd 2: Ch 3 (**counts as first dc**), dc in same st as joining, 2 dc in next dc and in each dc around; join with slip st to first dc: 24 dc.

Rnd 3 (Joining rnd)**:** Ch 2, with **wrong** side of both Flowers together, slip st in any ch-3 sp on **First Flower**, ch 1, slip st in next dc on **Second Flower**, ch 2, slip st in next ch-3 sp on **First Flower**, ch 1, slip st in next dc on **Second Flower**, (ch 3, slip st in next dc) 12 times, tie a scrap piece of thread around last ch-3 made for joining, ch 3, (slip st in next dc, ch 3) around; join with slip st to joining slip st at base of beginning ch-2, finish off: 24 sps.

THIRD FLOWER

With Lavender, ch 6; join with slip st to form a ring.

Rnd 1 (Right side)**:** Ch 3 (**counts as first dc**), 11 dc in ring; join with slip st to first dc: 12 dc.

Note: Mark Rnd 1 as **right** side.

Rnd 2: Ch 3 **(counts as first dc)**, dc in same st as joining, 2 dc in next dc and in each dc around; join with slip st to first dc: 24 dc.

Rnd 3 (Joining rnd)**:** Ch 2, with **wrong** sides of new Flower and previous Flower together, slip st in marked ch-3 sp on **previous Flower**, remove marker, ch 1, slip st in next dc on **new Flower**, ch 2, slip st in next ch-3 sp on **previous Flower**, ch 1, slip st in next dc on **new Flower**, (ch 3, slip st in next dc) 12 times, tie a scrap piece of thread around last ch-3 made for joining, ch 3, (slip st in next dc, ch 3) around; join with slip st to joining slip st at base of beginning ch-2, finish off: 24 sps.

FOURTH FLOWER

With Variegated, ch 6; join with slip st to form a ring.

Rnd 1 (Right side)**:** Ch 3 **(counts as first dc)**, 11 dc in ring; join with slip st to first dc: 12 dc.

Note: Mark Rnd 1 as **right** side.

Rnd 2: Ch 3 **(counts as first dc)**, dc in same st as joining, 2 dc in next dc and in each dc around; join with slip st to first dc: 24 dc.

Rnd 3 (Joining rnd)**:** Ch 2, with **wrong** sides of new Flower and previous Flower together, slip st in marked ch-3 sp on **previous Flower**, remove marker, ch 1, slip st in next dc on **new Flower**, ch 2, slip st in next ch-3 sp on **previous Flower**, ch 1, slip st in next dc on **new Flower**, (ch 3, slip st in next dc) 12 times, tie a scrap piece of thread around last ch-3 made for joining, ch 3, (slip st in next dc, ch 3) around; join with slip st to joining slip st at base of beginning ch-2, finish off: 24 sps.

FIFTH FLOWER

Work same as Third Flower.

SIXTH FLOWER

Work same as Fourth Flower through Rnd 2: 24 dc.

Rnd 3 (Joining rnd)**:** Ch 2, with **wrong** sides of new Flower and previous Flower together, slip st in marked ch-3 sp on **previous Flower**, remove marker, ch 1, slip st in next dc on **new Flower**, ch 2, slip st in next ch-3 sp on **previous Flower**, ch 1, slip st in next dc on **new Flower**, ch 3, (slip st in next dc, ch 3) around; join with slip st to joining slip st at base of beginning ch-2, finish off.

Using photo as a guide for placement, glue center of each Flower to ribbon; allow to dry completely. Trim ends as desired.

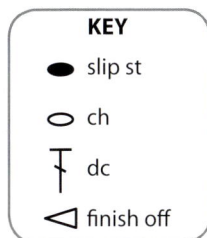

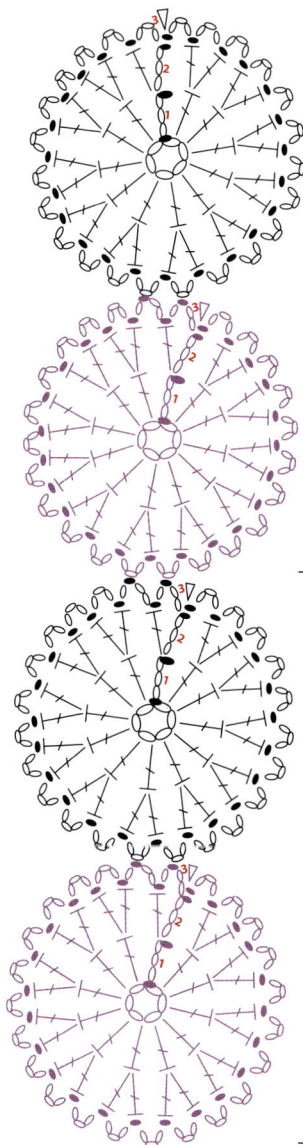

KEY

- ⬬ slip st
- ◯ ch
- ⊤ dc
- ◁ finish off

FIRST FLOWER

repeat one time

LOVING HEARTS

◖■■▢▢◗ EASY +

Approximate Finished Size:
1¾"w x 7"h (4.5 cm x 18 cm) (excluding ribbon)

SHOPPING LIST

Thread (Lace Weight) 🧶 0 LACE

Crochet Thread, size 10
[400 yards (366 meters) per ball **OR**
350 yards (320 meters) per ball]:
☐ White - 9 yards (8 meters)
☐ Pink - 8 yards (7.5 meters)

Crochet Hook
☐ Steel hook, size 10 (1.3 mm)

Additional Supplies
☐ 5/16"w (8 mm) Ribbon - 10" (25.5 cm) length

To make the Bookmark using the chart on page 35,
see Following Symbol Crochet Charts on page 46.

STITCH GUIDE

TREBLE CROCHET *(abbreviated tr)*

YO twice, insert hook in st indicated, YO and pull up a loop (4 loops on hook), (YO and draw through 2 loops on hook) 3 times.

INSTRUCTIONS

With White, ch 77.

Foundation Row: Dc in eighth ch from hook, ★ ch 2, skip next 2 chs, dc in next ch; repeat from ★ across: 24 dc and 24 sps.

Rnd 1 (Right side)**:** Ch 3 (**counts as first dc, now and throughout**), do **not** turn; 7 dc in sp at end of Foundation Row; working in sps of beginning ch, 2 dc in each of next 22 sps, 12 dc in sp at opposite end of Foundation Row, 2 dc in each of next 22 ch-2 sps, 4 dc in last ch-2 sp; join with slip st to first dc, finish off: 112 dc.

Note: Loop a short piece of thread around any stitch to mark Rnd 1 as **right** side.

Rnd 2: With **right** side facing, skip first 2 dc and join Pink with slip st in next dc; (ch 7, slip st in same st) twice, sc in next 6 dc, ★ slip st in next dc, (ch 7, slip st in same st) 3 times, sc in next 6 dc; repeat from ★ around, slip st in same st as joining, ch 3, tr in same st to form last ch-7 sp: 48 ch-7 sps.

Rnd 3: † (Ch 5, slip st in next ch-7 sp) twice, ch 8, slip st in next ch-7 sp, (ch 5, slip st in next ch-7 sp) 20 times, ch 8 †, slip st in next ch-7 sp, repeat from † to † once; join with slip st to tr at base of beginning ch-5, finish off.

Using photo as a guide, weave ribbon through sps on Foundation Row. Trim ends as desired.

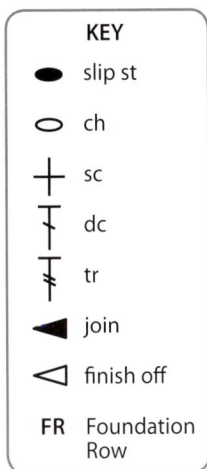

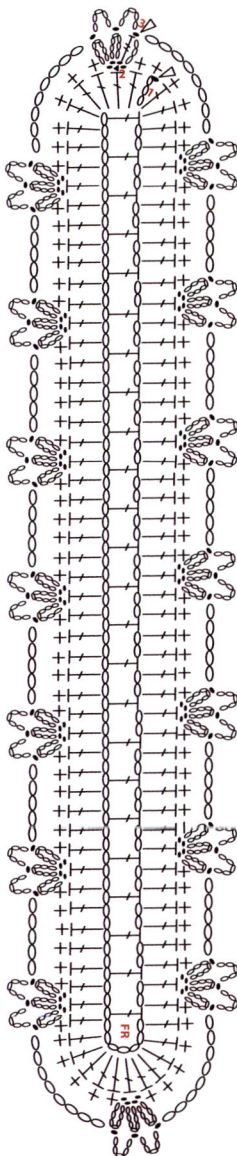

KEY	
●	slip st
○	ch
+	sc
†	dc
‡	tr
◀	join
◁	finish off
FR	Foundation Row

VICTORIAN LACE

◼◼◻◻ **EASY +**

Approximate Finished Size:
1 ¾"w x 7¼"h (4.5 cm x 18.5 cm) (excluding ribbon)

SHOPPING LIST

Thread (Lace Weight) **[LACE 0]**
Crochet Thread, size 10
[350 yards (320 meters) per ball]:
☐ 16 yards (14.5 meters)

Crochet Hook
☐ Steel hook, size 10 (1.3 mm)

Additional Supplies
☐ ¼"w (6 mm) Ribbon - 11" (28 cm) length

To make the Bookmark using the chart on page 39,
see Following Symbol Crochet Charts on page 46.

STITCH GUIDE

TREBLE CROCHET *(abbreviated tr)*
YO twice, insert hook in st indicated, YO and pull up a loop (4 loops on hook), (YO and draw through 2 loops on hook) 3 times.

INSTRUCTIONS

Ch 78.

Foundation Row: Tr in ninth ch from hook, ★ ch 2, skip next 2 chs, tr in next ch; repeat from ★ across: 24 tr and 24 sps.

Rnd 1 (Right side)**:** Ch 3 (**counts as first dc**), do **not** turn; dc in sp at end of Foundation Row, (ch 1, 2 dc in same sp) 3 times, working in sps of beginning ch, [dc in next sp, (2 dc, ch 1, 2 dc) in next sp] 11 times, 2 dc in sp at opposite end of Foundation Row, (ch 1, 2 dc in same sp) 5 times, [(2 dc, ch 1, 2 dc) in next ch-2 sp, dc in next ch-2 sp] 11 times, (2 dc, ch 1) twice in last ch-2 sp; join with slip st to first dc: 134 dc and 32 ch-1 sps.

Rnd 2: † Ch 7, skip next ch-1 sp and next dc, slip st in next dc, ch 7, skip next ch-1 sp, (slip st in next ch-1 sp, ch 7) 13 times, skip next ch-1 sp †, slip st in next dc, repeat from † to † once; join with slip st to joining slip st at base of beginning ch-7: 30 ch-7 sps.

Rnd 3: Ch 1, ★ 2 sc in next ch-7 sp, ch 5, [(slip st, ch 5) twice, 2 sc] in same sp; repeat from ★ around; join with slip st to first sc, finish off.

Using photo as a guide, weave ribbon through sps on Foundation Row.
Trim ends as desired.

KEY	
⬤	slip st
◯	ch
+	sc
†	dc
‡	tr
◁	finish off
FR	Foundation Row

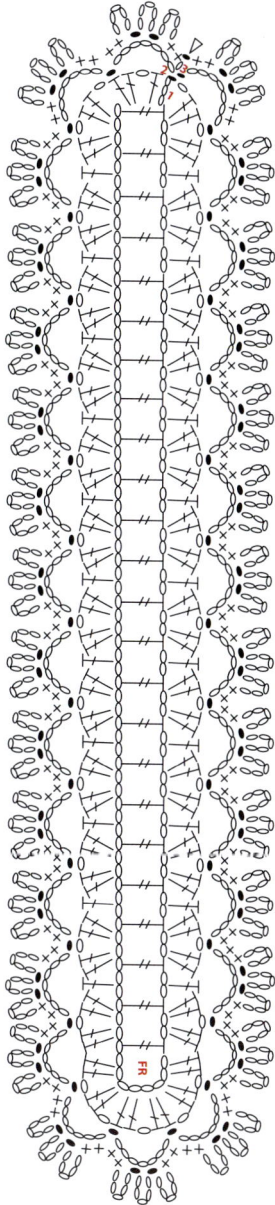

BERIBBONED CROSS

EASY +

Approximate Finished Size:
4⅜"w x 6"h (11 cm x 15 cm) (excluding ribbon)

SHOPPING LIST

Thread (Lace Weight) LACE 0
Crochet Thread, size 10
[350 yards (320 meters) per ball]:
☐ 10 yards (9 meters)

Crochet Hook
☐ Steel hook, size 10 (1.3 mm)

Additional Supplies
☐ ³/₈"w (10 mm) Ribbon - 16" (40.5 cm) length
☐ Craft glue

To make the Bookmark using the chart on page 43,
see Following Symbol Crochet Charts on page 46.

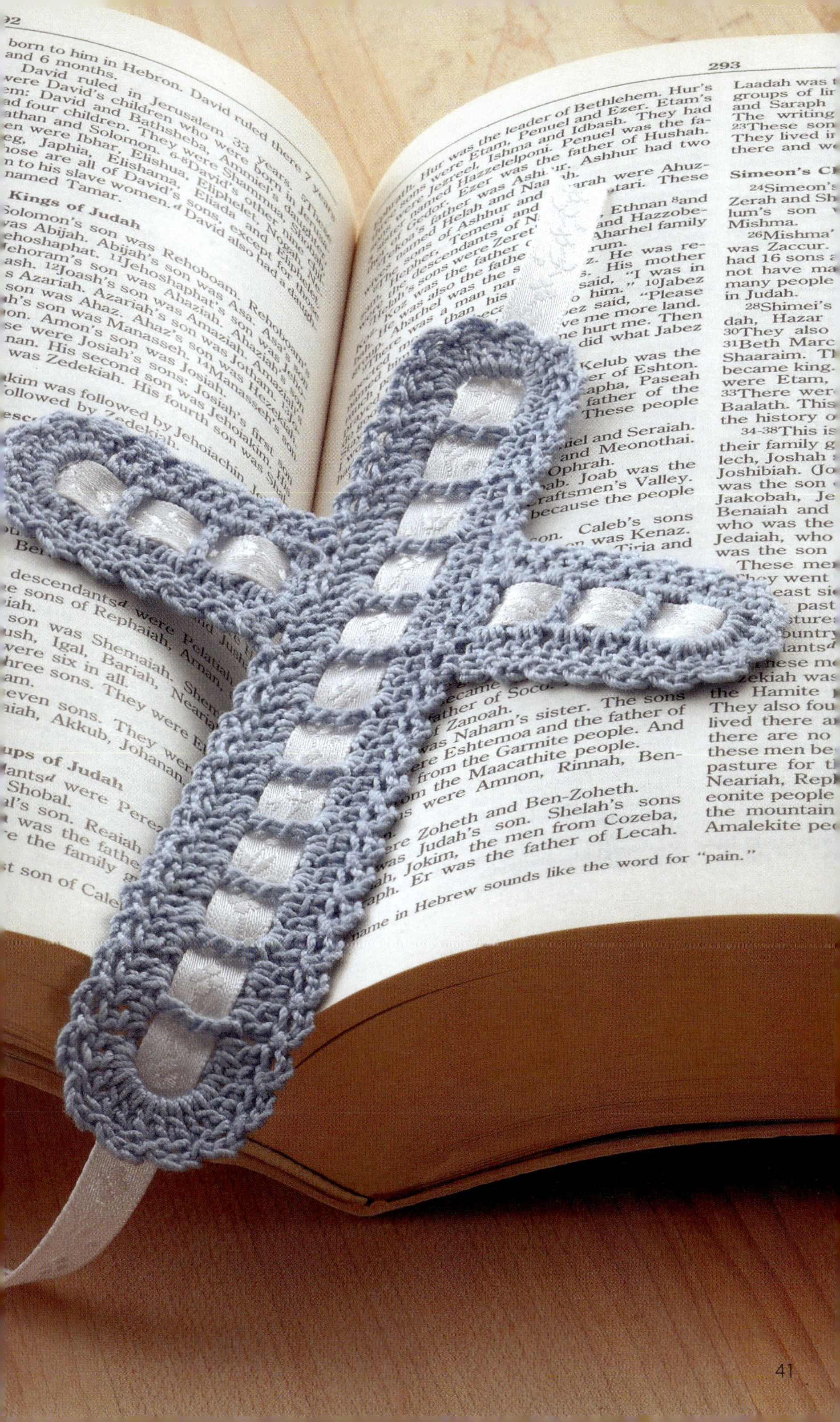

STITCH GUIDE

TREBLE CROCHET *(abbreviated tr)*
YO twice, insert hook in st indicated, YO and pull up a loop (4 loops on hook), (YO and draw through 2 loops on hook) 3 times.

INSTRUCTIONS
CENTER
Ch 78.

Foundation Row: Tr in ninth ch from hook, ★ ch 2, skip next 2 chs, tr in next ch; repeat from ★ across: 24 tr and 24 sps.

Rnd 1 (Right side)**:** Ch 3 (**counts as first dc**), do **not** turn; 7 dc in sp at end of Foundation Row, working in sps of beginning ch, 2 dc in each of next 22 sps, 12 dc in sp at opposite end of Foundation Row, 2 dc in each of next 22 ch-2 sps, 4 dc in last ch-2 sp; join with slip st to first dc: 112 dc.

Note: Loop a short piece of thread around any stitch to mark Rnd 1 as **right** side.

Rnd 2: Ch 3, skip next dc, ★ slip st in next dc, ch 3, skip next dc; repeat from ★ around; join with slip st to joining slip st at base of beginning ch-3, finish off: 56 ch-3 sps.

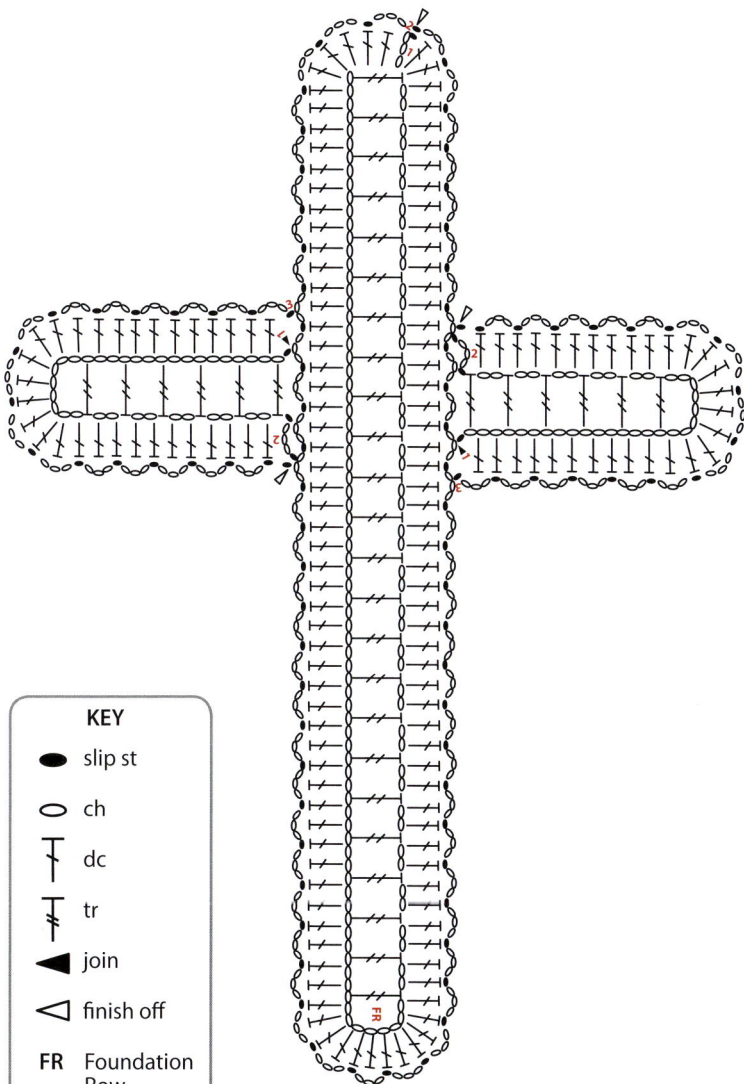

FIRST SIDE

SECOND SIDE

KEY

● slip st

○ ch

† dc

‡ tr

◀ join

◁ finish off

FR Foundation Row

FIRST SIDE

Row 1 (Foundation)**:** With **right** side facing, skip first 9 ch-3 sps of Center and join thread with slip st in next ch-3 sp; ch 24, tr in ninth ch from hook, ★ ch 2, skip next 2 chs, tr in next ch; repeat from ★ across; skip next ch-3 sp on Center, slip st in next ch-3 sp: 6 tr and 6 sps.

Row 2: Ch 3, slip st in next ch-3 sp on Center, **turn**; 2 dc in each of first 5 ch-2 sps, 10 dc in next sp (end of Foundation); working in sps of beginning ch, 2 dc in each of next 5 sps, slip st in next ch-3 sp on Center: 30 dc.

Row 3: Ch 3, turn; skip first dc, slip st in next dc, ★ ch 3, skip next dc, slip st in next dc; repeat from ★ across, slip st in same ch-3 sp on Center as first slip st on Row 2; finish off.

SECOND SIDE

Row 1 (Foundation)**:** With **right** side facing, skip next 32 unworked ch-3 sps of Center and join thread with slip st in next ch-3 sp; ch 24, tr in ninth ch from hook, ★ ch 2, skip next 2 chs, tr in next ch; repeat from ★ across; skip next ch-3 sp on Center, slip st in next ch-3 sp: 6 tr and 6 sps.

Rows 2 and 3: Work same as First Side.

Weave a 10" (25.5 cm) length of ribbon through sps on Foundation Row of Center; trim ends.
Weave a 3" (7.5 cm) length of ribbon through sps on Foundation Row of First Side, gluing each end on **wrong** side. Allow glue to dry completely.
Repeat on Second Side.

GENERAL INSTRUCTIONS

ABBREVIATIONS

ch(s)   chain(s)
cm   centimeters
dc   double crochet(s)
FR   Foundation Row
hdc   half double crochet(s)
mm   millimeters
Rnd(s)   Round(s)
sc   single crochet(s)
sp(s)   space(s)
st(s)   stitch(es)
tr   treble crochet(s)
YO   yarn over

CROCHET TERMINOLOGY	
UNITED STATES	INTERNATIONAL
slip stitch (slip st) =	single crochet (sc)
single crochet (sc) =	double crochet (dc)
half double crochet (hdc) =	half treble crochet (htr)
double crochet (dc) =	treble crochet(tr)
treble crochet (tr) =	double treble crochet (dtr)
double treble crochet (dtr) =	triple treble crochet (ttr)
triple treble crochet (tr tr) =	quadruple treble crochet (qtr)
skip =	miss

SYMBOLS & TERMS

★ — work instructions following ★ as many **more** times as indicated in addition to the first time.

† to † — work all instructions from first † to second † **as many** times as specified.

( ) or [ ] — work enclosed instructions **as many** times as specified by the number immediately following **or** work all enclosed instructions in the stitch or space indicated **or** contains explanatory remarks.

colon (:) — the number(s) given after a colon at the end of a row or round denote(s) the number of stitches or spaces you should have on that row or round.

STEEL CROCHET HOOKS														
U.S.	00	0	1	2	3	4	5	6	7	8	9	10	11	12	13	14
Metric - mm	3.5	3.25	2.75	2.25	2.1	2	1.9	1.8	1.65	1.5	1.4	1.3	1.1	1	.85	.75

◼◻◻◻ BEGINNER	Projects for first-time crocheters using basic stitches. Minimal shaping.
◼◼◻◻ EASY	Projects using yarn with basic stitches, repetitive stitch patterns, simple color changes, and simple shaping and finishing.
◼◼◼◻ INTERMEDIATE	Projects using a variety of techniques, such as basic lace patterns or color patterns, mid-level shaping and finishing.
◼◼◼◼ EXPERIENCED	Projects with intricate stitch patterns, techniques and dimension, such as non-repeating patterns, multi-color techniques, fine threads, small hooks, detailed shaping and refined finishing.

GAUGE

Our instructions are written for crochet thread, size 10. Gauge is not of great importance; your Bookmark may be a little larger or smaller without changing the overall effect.

FREE LOOPS OF A CHAIN

When instructed to work in free loops of a chain, work in loop indicated by arrow (Fig. 2).

Fig. 2

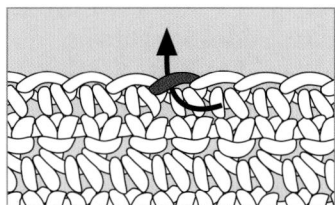

FOLLOWING SYMBOL CROCHET CHARTS

Symbols show the actual structure of a crochet design and each one represent a single specific stitch or where to join and finish off. A stitch is placed over the stitch or chain in which it is worked. Increases are shown with the correct number of stitches placed over one stitch. Our instructions provide written and symbol versions. They are both useful, even if you prefer one to the other. If you become confused following your preferred version, it is helpful to look at the other for clarification. Used together, they can answer almost any question you may have about a stitch or a pattern.

Yarn Weight Symbol & Names	LACE 0	SUPER FINE 1	FINE 2	LIGHT 3	MEDIUM 4	BULKY 5	SUPER BULKY 6
Type of Yarns in Category	Fingering, 10-count crochet thread	Sock, Fingering Baby	Sport, Baby	DK, Light Worsted	Worsted, Afghan, Aran	Chunky, Craft, Rug	Bulky, Roving
Crochet Gauge* Ranges in Single Crochet to 4" (10 cm)	32-42 double crochets**	21-32 sts	16-20 sts	12-17 sts	11-14 sts	8-11 sts	5-9 sts
Advised Hook Size Range	Steel*** 6,7,8 Regular hook B-1	B-1 to E-4	E-4 to 7	7 to I-9	I-9 to K-10.5	K-10.5 to M-13	M-13 and larger

*GUIDELINES ONLY: The chart above reflects the most commonly used gauges and hook sizes for specific yarn categories.

** Lace weight yarns are usually crocheted on larger-size hooks to create lacy openwork patterns. Accordingly, a gauge range is difficult to determine. Always follow the gauge stated in your pattern.

*** Steel crochet hooks are sized differently from regular hooks—the higher the number the smaller the hook, which is the reverse of regular hook sizing.

THREAD INFORMATION

Each Bookmark in this book was made using Aunt Lydia's® Crochet Thread, size 10. Any brand of lace weight thread may be used.

For your convenience, listed below are the specific colors used to create our photography models.

BIRDHOUSE BORDER
Purple Version
Purple - #458 Purple
Lavender - #495 Wood Violet
Variegated Version
#465 Pastel Ombre

BEAUTIFUL BUTTERFLY
Pink Version
Dk Pink - #493 French Rose
Pink - #4001 Orchid Pink
Blue Variegated Version
#14 Shaded Blues

LACY DREAM
#480 Delft

WOVEN CROSS
#495 Wood Violet

CROWNING TOUCH
#424 Peach

FANCIFUL FANS
#465 Pastel Ombre OR #423 Maize

PRESSED FLOWERS
Lavender - #495 Wood Violet
Variegated - 26 Shaded Purples

LOVING HEARTS
White - #1 White
Pink - #401 Orchid Pink

VICTORIAN LACE
#661 Frosty Green

BERIBBONED CROSS
#480 Delft

Your

PLEASE SHARE
your comments and suggestions at
www.facebook.com/Official.LeisureArts

PLUS you can find us on Twitter,
Pinterest, and YouTube!!

opinion matters!

We have made every effort to ensure that these instructions are accurate and complete. We cannot, however, be responsible for human error, typographical mistakes, or variations in individual work.

Production Team: Writer/Technical Editor - Linda A. Daley; Editorial Writer - Susan Frantz Wiles; Senior Graphic Artist - Lora Puls; Graphic Artist - Becca Snider Tally; Photo Stylist - Christy Meyers; and Photographer - Mark Mathews.